Outsourcing Technology in the Healthcare Industry: In-Depth Research to Protect the SECURITY, TECHNOLOGY, and PROFITABILITY of Your Business

Damon Clements

First Printing: 2016

ISBN 978-1-365-20682-5

Envisionet, LLC

704 S. State Road 135, Ste. D281

Greenwood, IN 46143

www.envisionetllc.com

Contents

To my wife Amber, my children Presley and Adalyn, and of course my amazingly supportive parents, David and Michele Clements. I wouldn't be where I am today if it wasn't for all of you!

Introduction

The Affordable Care Act (ACA) is one of the most polarizing and impactful pieces of legislation in recent history and the largest overhaul of the healthcare system in the last several decades. Along with this legislation came new mandates tied to financial incentives and penalties meant to pull more individuals into the healthcare system, drive down costs and improve outcomes. While many individuals and businesses were impacted by this legislation, healthcare organizations across the country assumed most of the burden to lower healthcare costs while finding ways to improve outcomes and the quality of care. Though a number of initiatives such as Electronic Medical Records (EMR), Computerized Provider Order Entry (CPOE), and electronic interfaces are being developed and pursued there are significant costs to implement, manage, and maintain these systems along with the costs associated with the management and maintenance of the day-to-day technology infrastructure.

For management, the concern is finding ways to implement and support the technology the organization needs, while doing so in the most cost-effective way in order to help drive down healthcare costs. While implementing an EMR may help create efficiencies and automate manual processes, it comes at a cost. If the costs of implementing and managing these technology systems outweigh or surpass the savings, then the organization may never realize their goal of reducing costs and improving care.

As someone who has worked as a technology professional and consultant to the healthcare industry for almost 20 years I have seen the technology challenges facing the average healthcare professional firsthand. This book is the culmination of years of experience, research and analysis of the costs and challenges to support increasingly complex technology solutions within the healthcare industry and the cost-benefit for an organization to incorporate an outsourcing strategy. Through this analysis, it is evident that there is significant demand for healthcare-specific IT consulting companies as well as significant benefit to healthcare organizations to partner with these organizations in order to address the specific challenges within the healthcare industry. The primary benefits to the healthcare organization will include lowering costs, improving efficiencies, and improving patient care and outcomes.

Section 1:

The Purpose Behind This Book

Since the passing of the Affordable Care Act, the healthcare industry has witnessed an unprecedented amount of change, innovation, and increased technological complexities. Healthcare organizations have been given the daunting task of reducing healthcare costs while at the same time improving quality of care and outcomes. As part of this initiative, the federal government has mandated the systematic adoption of Electronic Health Record (EHR) systems and participation in the Health Data Initiative, which requires providers to report on cost and quality data analytics (Silicon Valley, 2016).

For many healthcare organizations, the implementation of an EHR meant that technical staff were either going to need to develop a new set of skills or there would be significant additional costs to hire internal or external technicians to help them through the very complex implementation process. In addition to the implementation, providers would soon realize that there were ongoing support costs to consider. These systems needed to be backed up, upgraded, and continuously configured to meet evolving needs and requirements.

The Affordable Care Act alone does not account for all of the new technology challenges facing the healthcare industry today, rather a combination of factors. In part, the ACA became a catalyst for the creation of more than 500 new healthcare IT companies, along with new products and services that were meant to help the healthcare industry achieve their goals of better care, improved outcomes, and lower costs (Silicon Valley, 2016). Companies like Microsoft, IBM, Google, and Apple are all getting into the mix to develop new solutions and make their mark in this expanding healthcare technology market. Companies like these will become increasingly important as healthcare organizations continue to collect massive amounts of data and begin to ask questions that only the most sophisticated software and software developers can answer. Silicon Valley (2016) points out that globally, the healthcare IT market is expected to reach $105 billion by 2020, which is an increase from the $41 billion in 2013 and is powered by innovations in cloud technologies, clinical and claims based analytics, as well as mobile technologies. These new developments in mobile technology, wearable tech, data mining, and the ability to share and interface data across disparate systems has created increasing demand for the technical expertise needed to incorporate and support these innovations within the modern healthcare organization.

Increasing demand for experienced health IT professionals brings its own set of challenges. Perna, G. (2013) referenced a HIMSS Analytics Workforce Survey which indicated 31 percent of IT professionals had to put projects on hold due to staffing shortages, while 43 percent of providers and 56 percent of vendors cited a significant lack of qualified talent as their biggest challenge to staffing their environment. Healthcare organizations not only have unique technical challenges but have increasingly complex regulatory challenges to adhere to as well. These are significant factors which contribute to this talent shortage. Some organizations are able to internally train staff to take on new roles and responsibilities but others have been forced to look outside their organization and outsource this work.

As noted above, the changing healthcare industry has led to a proliferation of healthcare IT startups, products, and solutions which are all meant to help address the more modern challenges in the healthcare environment. However, these new technologies create their own set of challenges, many of which require a great deal of technical know-how that many healthcare organizations either do not have or cannot staff. This presents an opportunity that can benefit the healthcare industry as well as the technology consulting industry. EverestGroup stated that the healthcare provider segment is expected to experience the largest percentage in information technology outsourcing growth during 2014-2020 and new regulatory requirements, customer-centric care, and restructuring will help fuel the growth in the healthcare information technology outsourcing market (Everest Group, 2016).

While outsourcing can be a viable alternative for organizations who either struggle to find qualified talent or are looking for ways to cut costs, proper due diligence is necessary to help avoid many potential pitfalls. Even though IT consulting companies are prevalent in most areas, not all of them are experienced with the unique tools, challenges, and regulatory obligations typically found within in a healthcare setting. In fact, recently updated federal laws have made it even more important to ensure consulting companies are compliant with these regulations.

The Health Insurance Portability and Accountability Act (HIPAA) Omnibus rule was put into effect in the first quarter of 2013 and this has changed the scope and liability of protecting patient healthcare information and the access to it. The expansion of the HIPAA security rule meant that even if you are not a medical provider the security rule may still apply. For instance, any company who handles electronic medical records or otherwise does business with a healthcare organization will be required to comply with the security rule and must be fully HIPAA data security compliant (HIPAA, 2014). Based on first-hand experience with multiple IT consultants, this is not a well-known fact. Many IT consultants, healthcare providers, and healthcare organizations do not understand that partnering with a consultant who is not compliant with the HIPAA security rule is a compliance problem for which either party could be held liable in the event of a security breach. In fact, EverestGroup (2016) noted that any service provider who wishes to succeed in this market will need to focus on building expertise in this service line, develop and acquire talent and skills demanded by healthcare providers, and align themselves with the ever changing engagement models. This presents an opportunity for IT consulting companies who are able to gain and leverage their understanding and compliance with the healthcare industry.

The purpose of this book is to enhance the healthcare industry's understanding of the costs and benefits of outsourcing technology support and the need for more healthcare-specific IT consulting companies to adequately service these organizations. What will not be covered and is beyond the scope of this book is the outsourcing of other service lines, departments, or job functions. With respect to demand for technology support companies and their ability to effectively service the healthcare community, this study will focus on IT consulting agencies in the Indianapolis, Indiana area. Additionally, while much of this research is relevant to the healthcare industry as a whole, the focus with respect to IT consulting company knowhow and presence in the market will be limited to the Indianapolis area as well.

Section 2:

Why is This Significant to the Healthcare Industry?

Study of the technological challenges in the healthcare industry and the changing landscape as it pertains to healthcare IT outsourcing is essential. The Affordable Care Act was signed into law in 2010 and the healthcare industry is still in the very early stages of change and adoption. The full effect of these changes are years away from being completely understood or realized. Therefore, a great deal of additional study is needed to understand exactly how the changing technological landscape, along with this new law and its mandates will impact the healthcare industry from a technology and support perspective.

With so much new growth in the healthcare IT segment, there is increasing demand for the technical expertise to implement and support an ever increasing amount of technology innovations. Hospitals are under great demand to lower the overall cost of healthcare, produce better outcomes, and adopt many new technologies to support this. This puts greater pressure on these organizations to cut their operating costs and a solution to this problem may be to look outside of the organization and consider the advantages of outsourcing this work.

For most organizations, the decision to outsource has many potential advantages and disadvantages that are important to understand. Healthcare organizations have an increasing need to capture data, store the data, secure this data, mine the data, and share this data with a number of individuals and external organizations. New technologies are being developed at a rapid pace and healthcare organizations as well as providers are becoming increasingly reliant on these technologies. In addition, patients are increasingly demanding access to their own electronic health information and organizations must have the ability to respond quickly to these requests. Consequently, many healthcare organizations will consider outsourcing to third party healthcare IT (HIT) companies. That said, outsourcing has many consequences that are important to understand for the healthcare industry, the IT consulting industry, and the public at large.

This type of restructuring will impact quality, productivity, staff, the local community, and the financial health of the organization, making this decision significant to all stakeholders. Company leadership and stakeholders have a lot to gain or possibly lose if this process is not handled with a great deal of thought, communication, and strategic leadership. There are implications at the marketing level, ethical issues to consider, legal considerations, and broad impact on other industries, including the technology sector.

For the technology sector, specifically the healthcare IT support industry, the reason that healthcare organizations outsource is important to understand. If it is found that healthcare organizations outsource strictly to cut costs and save money, this will impact the HIT market in terms of the cost and type of support that is offered. Under this scenario, it may produce a more cost competitive market as HIT companies work to drive their costs down. Conversely, if it is found that healthcare organizations outsource primarily to improve quality, performance, and attain a greater ability to adapt to the changing technology landscape, HIT support companies might be more inclined to offer unique and specialized services that are more focused on helping the healthcare organization meet their goals.

Having worked in the healthcare industry in a technology support capacity for over fifteen years, this is an important area of study for me in particular. There are broad implications on future job opportunities, the structure of the healthcare industry, along with financial ramifications that impact both the organization and the income of current or future employees. In addition, there is evidence to suggest that new opportunities may present themselves in the form of technology consulting and general education for the healthcare community.

Many IT support companies are not equipped or knowledgeable of many of the specific technical challenges or regulatory challenges that are unique to the healthcare industry. The healthcare organizations themselves do not always understand who they are doing business with and may not necessarily understand the type of help they need or who they really should be getting it from. Changes in the law along with changes in the technology sector can be difficult to navigate and forming partnerships with key consulting partners will be a key component of success for healthcare organizations.

Working with healthcare organizations to guide them through the process of selecting appropriate technical solutions to their challenges is important to me for many reasons. I sincerely believe that providing specialized support is the best way to help these organizations begin to lower the cost of technology support and implementation. This in turn will help drive down costs and will put the organization in a position to provide improved care through increased technology efficiencies.

Section 3:

The Changing Healthcare Landscape

In a 2012 budget statement put forth by Health and Human Services (HHS) Secretary, Kathleen Sebelius, she summarized the agency's mission to strengthen healthcare; advance scientific knowledge and innovation; advance the health, safety and well-being of the American people; and do this efficiently, transparently, and with accountability (Robeznieks, 2013). In many ways this encapsulates the enormous impact of the Affordable Care Act and the type of change that began with its implementation which continues today. This initiative has changed healthcare in ways that will not be completely realized for years to come.

For decades, the healthcare industry has operated under a volume based, fee-for-service model. This profitability model focused on getting patients in and out of the doctor's office as quickly as possible. Under this model, providers would get reimbursed for the work performed regardless of any improvement in outcome or quality of work performed. With the passing of the Affordable Care Act, this is all set to change. In 2015 roughly 20% of Medicare payments to providers are linked to programs which are designed to boost quality and reduce overall costs according to the Centers for Medicare and Medicaid Services (Cheney, 2015). This is a major shift in payment model which requires major changes in the health systems and technology.

As an example of the type of change that will become more prevalent in the industry, Dartmouth-Hitchcock has invested heavily into technologies such as telemedicine. A recent partnership with the Mayo Clinic in Arizona led to the development of a patient portal, providing 24/7 access to individual neurological assessments for patients and through developments such as these, the organization was able to free up more of their beds through improved technological capabilities (Cheney, 2015). This case is an illustration of the importance and significance of healthcare IT in today's value based model.

Dartmouth-Hitchcock was able to utilize advances in healthcare technology to create new efficiencies that will help them to provide better care to their patients. Electronic Medical Record systems, Computerized Physician Order Entry, and digital pathology for primary diagnosis are examples of other advances in technology that are sure to further revolutionize the healthcare industry. At the same time however, these technologies increase the complexity of the healthcare technology landscape and lead to an increased need for technical experts to manage such technologies.

In addition to leveraging technology to create efficiencies and improve patient care, providers need to have real metrics that they can report on. Healthcare organizations have an obligation and a need to track clinical data, status of the patient, experience of care and obtain real time data along with monthly aggregate data. Equally important, they must possess the ability to drill down into this data effectively (Cheney, 2015). This means that not only does the right data need to be captured electronically but the analytical expertise and technology support to retrieve it is vital as well.

Technology continues to advance in the areas of improved healthcare systems and reporting but so too are the tools and services used by the average patient. New technological trends such as social media, smart phones, tablets, and cloud technology are revolutionizing the industry. These technologies are arming patients with new and improved ways to research their healthcare as well as how they correspond with their providers. Patients are turning to these tools to find information on clinical trials, locating a doctor, finding educational material, and increasingly provided access to their specific results and medical histories. Healthcare organizations must become proficient in these technologies and understand how to use them safely and securely to meet not only the needs of their patients but also meet their regulatory and legal obligations.

There are many new laws and mandates that the healthcare organization must be mindful of in order to operate within the law and adequately protect the private patient data that they collect. Navigating through all of these regulations and tools and doing so in a cost-effective manner can be a daunting challenge. Not only is this challenging for the healthcare organizations but the service providers and technology consultants who work with them must be well versed in these tools and regulations as well.

Healthcare organizations without the budget or the staff to take advantage of some of the advances in technology are missing a big opportunity to create new efficiencies and reductions in cost. For many of these organizations, this presents an opportunity to outsource staff, move to the cloud, or both. Temkar, (2015) points out that many life sciences organizations could save up to 25% of their annual operating expenditure on clinical IT systems through the use of cloud computing technology as it can reduce costs, automate systems, provide remote access, and increase flexibility. The benefits of outsourcing technology services and movement to the cloud can help healthcare organizations achieve their goals of reduced cost and improved care. As such, there continues to be a trend in moving non-core services and staff out of the organization and moving these functions to third party providers and consultants. In fact, outsourcing may lead to reduced capital expenditures and allow the organization to focus more specifically on its core activities. Equally important, organizations must partner with appropriate technology partners in order to streamline their processes (Temkar, P., 2015).

As previously stated, the purpose of this book is to enhance the healthcare industry's understanding of the costs and benefits of outsourcing technology support and the need for more healthcare-specific IT consulting companies to adequately service these organizations. This book and the research within is therefore significant in many key areas. Solutions to the healthcare technology challenges of today and of tomorrow indicate that outsourcing non-core services such as the information technology support within the organization have many advantages to the bottom-line and to the quality and outcomes of the care provided. Moving services to the cloud or to technology consulting partners has significant impact on the healthcare industry and downstream partners and industries as well.

The technology industry in general must understand the trends and goals of the healthcare industry in order to develop and innovate in ways that are positively impactful to those goals. Likewise, the IT support industry must develop and mature to more effectively support these goals and initiatives. While many IT support organizations exist today and service many different industries, the healthcare industry is distinctly unique. Therefore, the IT support industry needs to adapt and become knowledgeable in the industry and ensure that they too follow appropriate regulatory obligations and speak to their understanding and accountability.

Section 4:

What You as a Healthcare Leader Should Consider

With so much change still taking place in the healthcare industry, specifically as it relates to new and developing technology challenges, there are a multitude of issues for healthcare organizations and leaders of these organizations to consider. Additionally, the IT support industry needs to educate themselves in the specific challenges and legal obligations that now apply to them and their business partners when supporting these organizations.

When considering how to best manage the ever changing and increasingly complex technology landscape, healthcare organizations must face the possibility that outsourcing may be the optimal strategy. In order to outsource effectively however, much care should be given to the approach. In particular, healthcare organizations who currently staff technology support teams must weigh the advantages against the disadvantages. Certainly there are cost considerations to take into account but in addition to this, there is an ethical element in making a decision like this. The elimination of jobs not only has an impact on a person's livelihood but also has impact on the rest of the organization as well as the local community. Communication is essential when working through this process, along with having a clear strategy on dealing with employee morale, concerns, and questions.

The employee element brings with it certain ethical considerations but so too does the decision on who to partner with or outsource to. Healthcare organizations may be tempted to simply select the organization that has the lowest pricing or perhaps choose an organization based on personal relationships. The question they must ask themselves is whether this is the best decision for the health of their organization, the reputation of their practice and most important of all, the safety of their patients. When partnering with an outsourcing provider healthcare organizations must take great care to ensure that the IT support organization demonstrates an understanding of their specific needs and perhaps most importantly, meets their respective legal and compliance obligations.

IT support organizations who service the healthcare industry must also be cognizant of their moral, ethical and legal obligation to represent themselves accurately. Many IT support organizations will market and promote themselves within the healthcare market but show no observable understanding or representation of their regulatory obligations, specifically as it pertains to HIPAA. In fact, according to Health and Human Services, it is incumbent upon the healthcare organization to obtain satisfactory assurances from their business associates they will appropriately handle and safeguard the protected health information they may store, transmit, or create on behalf of the healthcare organization.

What many healthcare organizations and IT support providers do not realize is that the law as it pertains to business associates recently changed in a very significant way. This change was known as the final rule or Omnibus rule. The U.S. Department of Health and Human Services released the final rule in early 2013 and set the compliance date for September of the same year (HIPAA, 2014). The most significant aspect of this final rule had to do with the responsibilities of subcontractors. Historically, IT support organizations would have signed a Business Associate agreement between themselves and the healthcare organization, also known as a covered entity. This would create a legal obligation to protect patient information between the covered entity and the IT support company. The IT support company would be known as a business associate of the covered entity. However, these IT support companies often have subcontractors of their own and may provide access to patient information indirectly through these relationships.

The final rule now places responsibility and liability directly on the business associate as well as their subcontractors. Meaning, many of the provisions of the HIPAA Privacy Rule and all aspects of the Security Rule now apply to both the business associate and their subcontractors and require them to have agreements with each other when accessing or handling protected health information (HIPAA, 2014).

With so much impacting the healthcare industry today in terms of regulatory obligations and the changing technology environment, there are several key questions that are worthy of further exploration and understanding. The following questions have therefore been addressed in order to evaluate and understand outsourcing technology support in the healthcare industry and whether the IT support industry is adequately equipped to handle these needs:

1. **Is outsourcing technology support within a healthcare organization a more efficient and cost-effective strategy?**

   This is a fundamental question that many healthcare organizations have either already determined, are in the process of determining, or have likely considered at one point or another. Healthcare organizations are in the business of patient care. They have mandates to reduce costs and improve outcomes. These mission-centric goals can only be achieved through the proper utilization of modern day technologies. In order to implement and support these technologies in the most cost-effective manner, the organization must consider current and future support costs, staffing challenges, internal payroll budgets, internal vs. external expertise, and understand the advantages or disadvantages at an operational and productivity level. This research will help reveal the costs and benefits of an outsourcing strategy in the healthcare industry.

2. **What technology roles might make better candidates to outsource? Infrastructure? Security? Core application support?**

When it comes to outsourcing, there are many possible strategies to consider. Many Electronic Medical Record vendors will offer hosted platforms, which eliminates the burden to house and maintain expensive IT equipment to support these vital systems. Amazon and Microsoft offer cloud computing services, allowing organizations to move servers and desktops into the cloud. This strategy effectively serves to outsource much cost and maintenance overhead of the hardware for critical infrastructure components. Security is another key technology component that must be properly administered and is critical in a healthcare environment. We are now seeing organizations begin to staff Chief Security Officers, a relatively new role in the industry. Many small to medium sized businesses are at a distinct disadvantage however, as they do not have the funds to staff an individual who focuses solely on security. With security threats becoming increasingly prevalent and easier to widely distribute, it is more important than ever to ensure adequate attention is paid to this area of technology support. Often, this can be done in a very cost effective way through an outsourcing arrangement. The day-to-day support of infrastructure such as routine maintenance, backups, desktop support, and print management is another key area to consider. All of these areas and more can be outsourced, ad-hoc, or the entire technology support system may be moved externally. Is one strategy more advantageous than another? This is another question to be answered as we work our way through the research.

3. **What are the responsibilities of the healthcare organization and ethical considerations when considering an outsourcing strategy?**
Making the decision to outsource is a complex and potentially challenging decision that may have far reaching effects on other areas of the business. Leadership within the organization have certain responsibilities to the patients they serve, the employees they hire, and the communities they operate in. An outsourcing strategy must take all of this into account and understanding what specific considerations must be factored in to a decision like this will be brought forth through this study.

4. **Are there enough healthcare IT support organizations to handle the demand?**
There are countless numbers of quality technology support organizations in almost every community. What is not clear however, is what percentage of those are actually qualified and experienced support providers for the healthcare

industry. Many technology support providers work with healthcare organizations but are they doing so in a compliant manner? Are they transparent when selling their services to healthcare organizations and work to educate their prospective customers on the responsibility they and their subcontractors have to protect patient data? Are there enough healthcare technology support providers in the local communities to support this need? This book will work to answer this question.

5. **What are the ethical and legal obligations of IT support organizations who solicit business from healthcare organizations?**

Just because you can do something, doesn't necessarily mean that you should. This is true in the case of technology support providers. Just because they can handle most or all of an organization's technology challenges and convince a healthcare organization to partner with them, doesn't mean the partnership is in the best interest of the healthcare organization or the support provider. There are serious potential legal and financial penalties for both organizations if certain obligations are not met. This presents ethical, moral, and even legal considerations that must be factored in, prior to forming such a partnership. This book will work to outline these considerations in clear detail.

4.1: Points of Reference

The data utilized throughout my research and construction of this book was obtained through multiple sources. Industry information concerning healthcare and the impact of the Affordable Care Act along with HIPAA regulatory mandates were obtained from online publications from the U.S. Department of Health and Human Services. Other publications and peer reviewed articles on this subject were obtained from the Indiana Wesleyan Off Campus Library Services (OCLS) website.

Certain variables investigated through my research including the costs and benefits of a technology outsourcing strategy were obtained from the OCLS website. Cost variables investigated in this book include the costs associated with outsourcing technology support and the overhead costs involved in managing and maintaining an in-house technology staff. The overhead costs include salaries of staff, training, office space, and computer equipment. Outsourcing costs will include the hard costs to obtain third party support as well as some of the intangible costs of outsourcing to a technology support company. These intangible costs include limitations of the technology support provider, quality of support, knowledge of the healthcare industry, and potential legal or financial penalties.

Benefits that result from outsourcing to a technology support organization will be investigated in this book as well and in some cases are not as easily quantified as the costs. In many respects, the true benefits, such as improved patient outcomes, may not be seen until well after the initial investment is made to outsource technology support. However, benefits will include efficiencies gained, money saved through elimination of staff, and increased ability to react and leverage changes in technology.

To get a sense for what is happening in the technology support industry in major metropolitan cities and their support of healthcare organizations, Indianapolis, Indiana was selected as a sample for the purposes of this research. Industry information was obtained for the technology support sector to determine the general availability of technology support companies in the Indianapolis area and what percentage of those specialize in healthcare support. Of those companies who represent themselves as supporting the healthcare industry, the percentage of those organizations who claim to be HIPAA compliant, willing to sign business associate agreements, or show a significant level of experience or understanding of the industry will be determined. This information will be collected from private company websites, the Indianapolis Chamber of Commerce, search engine results, and library resources.

Section 5:

What the Research Has to Say

Since the passing of the Affordable Care Act, the healthcare industry has been working through a great deal of change. A good majority of this change and the ability to meet new regulatory obligations will require healthcare organizations to adopt and become more proficient with technology. There are significant advantages to outsourcing some or all of this support and a growing demand for healthcare IT support organizations to meet this need. A good deal of the available literature on this subject focuses on the decision-making process, outsourcing benefits such as improved efficiencies and the impact on quality of care.

5.1: History of Technology in the Healthcare Industry

The healthcare industry is in a constant state of change and has been throughout history. Educational requirements have been improved; there have been significant advances in the area of pharmaceuticals and the discovery of vaccines; there have been advances in sterilization techniques, improvement in quality of care and procedures, and significant advancements in the area of technology (Sheingold & Hahn, 2014).

Advancements in technologies, techniques, and procedures eventually led to a need to develop a set of standards. The College of American Pathologists began to work toward a nomenclature of pathology reporting in 1965, which is now internationally recognized, while standards for laboratory message exchange, properties for electronic health record systems, data content, and health information system security standards were also developed. (Evolution, n.d.) As these standards began to develop in the healthcare industry, the American National Standards Institute (ANSI) was created to act as a form of coordination point for healthcare informatics standards (Evolution, n.d.). These standards were meant to not only help the medical community speak in similar terms and techniques but equally as important, these standards were developed to help address advancements in technology systems and the need to create efficient and secure means to communicate and interface data electronically.

As more healthcare organizations begin to adopt Electronic Medical Record Systems, there is an increased need to send and receive data from many different information systems. As an example, hospitals may utilize a laboratory system from one vendor, a pharmacy system from another, and a patient care system from yet another vendor (Evolution, n.d.). In addition to this, physicians or other organizations affiliated with these hospitals have unique systems of their own and often require access to data from the hospital in order to treat their patients (Evolution, n.d.).

As previously stated, perhaps the most significant event to occur in the healthcare industry in recent history was the passing of the Affordable Care Act. This new law brought millions of additional patients into the system and emphasized the adoption and implementation of healthcare information technology solutions. In fact, the entire concept of the ACA in terms of healthcare reform is dependent upon the development, collection, and sharing of information made possible through advancements in healthcare information technology (Fontenot, S. F., 2014).

What has become evident over the past several decades is the increasing reliance on technology and the increasing complexity of these systems and the issues surrounding them. Smart IT governance is a key component to successfully navigating through these technology challenges. "Implementation of ACA's voluminous regulations may always be a moving target. Implementation dates, reporting deadlines and even the requirements themselves are constantly shifting. The more flexible an employer's technology can be, the more effectively it can meet these challenges" (Horalek, P., 2014, p. 35). I would add to this that in an industry in a constant state of change, it is more important than ever to have trusted partners to guide the healthcare organization through the maze of technology solutions and regulatory considerations.

5.2: Outsourcing Technology Support

"Outsourcing allows organizations to upgrade their IT platforms using operating budgets, not capital budgets...and applications can easily be delivered via the cloud, which relieves the organization of all the maintenance, updates and security issues" (ZIMLICH, R., 2015, p. 2). With so much emphasis being placed on the technology capabilities in the modern healthcare organization, having a strategy to manage technology in an efficient, and cost-effective manner is more important than ever. As a result, many healthcare organizations have turned toward various forms of outsourcing to mitigate risk, cut costs, or to simply have the flexibility and depth of expertise that may best be found with a good outsourcing partner. It is important to understand the many costs and benefits of this strategy. While outsourcing may be significantly advantageous to healthcare organizations, there are several considerations that must be taken into account, which we will review now.

Applied Management Theory

When making a decision as significant as outsourcing, there are strategic discussions that will take place at multiple levels of the organization. Bateman, T.S., & Snell, S.A. (2013) describe how group discussions are advantageous as they can significantly improve the chances that sound decision making will take place and that the end result will be of much higher quality. This decision-making strategy helps to ensure that multiple perspectives are considered and that biases are mitigated. Paul, R., & Elder, L.,

(2014) talk about fairness and our tendency to think from a perspective that benefits ourselves. It is easy to form a bias in situations like these and possibly think selfishly about what is best for the organization. Forming a strategic group to work through the decision-making process is one effective way to mitigate biases and build a consensus that is in the best interest of the organization and the patients they serve.

Ethics and Legal Aspects of Management

As noted above, making the decision to outsource a critical business function such as technology support has both financial implications and staffing implications. In addition to this, there are significant ethical and moral considerations to take into account when working through the outsourcing decision-making process. This type of process may look similar to the one described by Collins, D. (2009) who outlines an ethical decision making framework that consists of a set of six questions to evaluate the ethical nature of the decision. Who will be affected? Is the action beneficial to you personally? Is the action supported by your social group? Is the action supported by national laws? Is the decision for the greatest good of the greatest number of people affected? Lastly, are the motives behind the action based on truthfulness and respect of all stakeholders?

Using this type of framework and making sure to ask the right questions with respect to the ethical and legal aspects of a decision like this is vital. While this seems simple on its surface, starting with a simple framework will often lead to a deeper set of questions and discussions that will get to the heart of the ethical and legal concerns that must be carefully reviewed.

Decision Making and Essential Business Communication

Several factors and issues lead to an organization's decision to outsource. O'Rourke, J., IV. (2013) suggest that one must first identify the issue, be specific about the desired change, and finally, state the benefits of making the proposed change. One of the primary issues in the healthcare industry has to do with profits. The Affordable Care Act is mandating the implementation and use of more technology solutions, which costs a great deal of money to purchase, implement, and maintain. Additionally, there are new payment models in development, which emphasizes outcomes instead of volumes. "Players in the healthcare industry are having their profits squeezed and the sad reality is that many are on the brink of failure as a result" (Parmar, P., 2015, p. 1). The pressure and strain from these external forces have forced many healthcare providers to sell their business or partner with larger businesses just to stay afloat (Parmar, P., 2015). Outsourcing non-medical business functions to external third party providers have therefore been an attractive alternative for many providers.

Leadership and Organizational Change

In the world of business, decision making is not always "black or white". What we find very often are situations where we must choose between two "rights" or what are called ethical dilemmas (Hughes, et al, 2012). Outsourcing is one such ethical dilemma in terms of the right course of action for the business versus the best course of action for staff and the livelihood of individuals impacted by such a decision.

As a business leader, you must be able to make the tough choices and do so in a professional and ethical way. The decision to outsource or not to outsource has serious ramifications. Even if jobs are not replaced, the decision to hand over a critical business function such as the security and reliability of your technology can be a frightening prospect but it doesn't need to be. Provided appropriate due diligence is exercised when selecting a partner an effective technology support provider could open up a wealth of opportunities and reveal cost savings and efficiencies that might not have been possible otherwise.

Business Strategy and Policy

The PESTEL model is a framework that categorizes and analyzes external factors such as political, economic, sociocultural, technological, ecological, and legal, which may serve to create opportunities or threats for an organization. The key take-away from the five forces model is that the stronger (weaker) the forces, the lower (greater) the industry's ability to earn above-average profits, and correspondingly, the lower (greater) the firm's ability to gain and sustain a competitive advantage (Rothaermel, 2015). The healthcare industry has been under increasingly stronger political, economic, legal, and technological forces in recent years. This has made it even more difficult to create and sustain profitability. As noted previously, many healthcare providers have been forced to give up their independent status and affiliate or sell their business to larger businesses just to make ends meet. Outsourcing non-core functions such as technology support has become a potential solution to this problem. A challenge to outsourcing that must be considered however, is whether the outsourcing partner is qualified and knowledgeable with respect to supporting the technology needs of the healthcare industry. If you are able to do this prior to engaging in a contractual situation with a technology provider, you can save yourself a lot of grief and heartache as unraveling these relationships can be a daunting challenge.

Marketing Considerations

Unethical selling can come in many forms and can sometimes be very hard to detect. Often there are details purposely hidden in the "fine text" of a contract or in an ad or article describing the promotion. For many, this is often not realized until after it is too late and the purchase has already been made. Other times, unethical selling comes in the form of just sheer misrepresentation. These sales tactics are often a result of fierce or unethical competitive practices that pressure the salesperson into misbehaving in order to remain competitive (Serviere-Munoz, L., & Mallin, M. L., 2013).

Technology support organizations are no different and there is the potential that they may not represent themselves appropriately. Pratt, M. K. (2008) point out that more organizations are looking at the ethics statements of the companies they do business with to ensure their statements are in alignment with the morals and ethics of the organization. Examining a provider's social policies has business value as ethical labor practices translates into better employee retention and improved engagement (Pratt, M. K., 2008).

Take care to ask potential partners the tough questions to ensure they not only have the expertise to support your business but do so in a way that makes sense to your bottom line. Is all on-site and off-site work covered as part of the monthly agreement? Are hourly rates incurred after a certain number of hours are exceeded? Are their business hours consistent with your business hours or will you be charged higher rates because you open or close at different hours? Are they compliant with the HIPAA security rule? Can they provide any evidence of this compliance? These are just some of the questions you should be asking prospective support providers to ensure they are representing themselves appropriately and that their business aligns with yours.

Section 6:

Healthcare IT Support Industry Analysis

For years, healthcare companies received technology support from in-house staff, vendor partners, or some form of external technology consulting provider. By and large, this is still true today. However, the introduction of HIPAA changed the nature of these relationships forever.

Prior to the introduction of HIPAA, encryption was a concept that almost no healthcare company was familiar with, let alone utilizing. Part of this had to do with the technology limitations of the day and another part was simply due to the fact that it was not a requirement and would have been more trouble than it was worth for most organizations.

The changing healthcare laws and advancements in technology has changed all of that. Now, it is a requirement that protected health information is encrypted and additionally, it is a requirement that all business associates who handle, create or have regular contact with this data be compliant with the HIPAA security rule and portions of the privacy rule and practice the same level of security and care with the data as the businesses they serve.

Where I see a significant challenge for the healthcare industry is in finding technology support organizations that truly understand the healthcare industry, have a clear focus on serving this industry, and fully understand and align themselves with the unique challenges and compliance obligations that continue to evolve every day.

Manta.com is an online search engine and comprehensive database of individual businesses. They have millions of unique visitors every month and provide a listing of businesses in specific industry segments and specific geographic locations (Manta.com., n.d.). According to Manta.com (n.d.), there are over 8000 companies listed under "computer consulting" in the Indianapolis area. When refining this search to "healthcare computer consulting" the results drop to just over 500. Upon review of the first 100 companies in that list of 500, there were no technology support companies dedicated to supporting the healthcare industry. A small percentage of the companies listed did note healthcare as an industry they serviced. However, they did not speak to specifics with regard to their understanding of HIPAA or their understanding and accountability to be compliant themselves.

Annette Porter, Orion HealthCorp Client Relations Manager noted several key concerns when partnering with an organization to outsource technology. In particular, Annette noted the possible lack of understanding on the part of the IT consulting company on certain workflows and healthcare related problems as well as concerns about transparency. "How do we really know they are HIPAA compliant and that the risk is minimal" (A. Porter, personal communication, February 29, 2016)? John Challenger, CEO of Challenger, Gray & Christmas In., a Chicago-based outplacement firm noted that "For the health care industry, there will be a large amount of work that will be flowing in their doors, and there will be new kinds of companies and services emerging. It's the perfect time for a new kind of expert to come in and offer support. When there is a sea change, there are also lots of opportunities" (Pyrillis, R., 2014, para. 4).

Section 7:

The Costs and Benefits of Outsourcing IT

In order to best determine the costs and benefits of outsourcing technology support a full cost-benefit analysis has been conducted. A cost-benefit analysis is the process of outlining general strengths and weaknesses of a project or decision in order to determine the value of the decision and establish whether or not they are worthwhile endeavors. Under this analysis, the benefits must outweigh the costs within a reasonable amount of time in order for the approach to be worthwhile. This analysis will determine whether outsourcing technology support is a sound financial and strategic decision for a typical healthcare organization and whether more healthcare specific technology support companies are needed to meet the demand.

To understand what type of healthcare organizations would outsource technology support and the demand for support providers, demographic data was analyzed. The most likely organizations to outsource would be those who are under great pressure to cut costs, companies who do not have internal expertise to effectively support current systems, or those who wish to adapt more quickly to changes in technologies and are actively considering the purchase of new technologies. Additionally, smaller organizations will tend to outsource nearly all of their IT operations, while midsize organizations tend to support technology internally, and larger organizations engage more frequently in partial outsourcing (Eddy, N., 2014).

According to Worldwide (2016), "global IT spending is forecast to grow from $2.46 trillion in 2015 to more than $2.8 trillion in 2019", citing healthcare as the fastest growing vertical industry through this period (para. 1). An annual outsourcing survey conducted between 2010 and 2011 cited a "13.1% growth rate for the top 20 outsourcing firms who support healthcare companies and a client base that grew from 14,556 to 16,463" (Kutscher, B., 2012, para. 3). The same survey concluded that outsourcing is occurring in large healthcare organizations, independent hospitals and small medical facilities.

According to search results from Manta.com (n.d.), there are over 12,000 healthcare organizations and over 8000 companies listed under "computer consulting" in the Indianapolis area. When refining this search to "healthcare computer consulting" the results drop to just over 500. Upon review of the first 100 companies in that list of 500, there were no technology support companies dedicated to supporting the healthcare industry.

A study of more than 5,000 health plans revealed, "40% of small-to-medium-sized plans outsource some portion of their operation compared to 20% in 2013" (ZIMLICH, R., 2015, p. 1). In addition to this, another study shows that "approximately 38% of organizations outsourced at least some portion of technology support" (Help Desk., 2014, p. 4). Using this data and the estimated number of healthcare organizations in the Indianapolis area, the conclusion is that approximately 4,800 healthcare companies in the area are either currently outsourcing some portion of their technology support or may be open to that possibility.

7.1: Cost of Outsourcing Technology Support

The process of outsourcing technology support and partnering with a technology support organization can be very costly. There are many things for a healthcare organization to consider when determining how and if to outsource technology support. Depending on the type of support that is outsourced there are typically monthly fees that must be considered and budgeted for as an ongoing expense. Although those expenses may be cheaper month-to-month than staffing a full IT department, there are often significant costs that are not altogether obvious when entering into a support contract. For instance, there may be a large initial up-front cost to cover the transition. Additionally, there may be hidden hourly fees that are often unpredictable to cover work that goes above and beyond the outsourcing agreement. Intangible costs such as response times are often overlooked as well. If the healthcare organization outsources the help desk function for example and internal staff get much slower responses to their technical issues, the company stands to lose a great deal of productivity.

Another potential hidden cost has to do with the retention of internal IT staff. What organizations hope to achieve in many cases is full outsourcing of technology support without the need to carry internal staff. However, Han, K., & Mithas, S. (2013) point out that no matter how well designed a contract may be, a firm may still need some level of in-house technology expertise in order to ensure the firm's interests are placed ahead of the vendor's and to help translate the functional domain knowledge of the internal business into language and technical specifications that the outsourcing partner can understand. While this may not be possible for all organizations, it highlights the importance of partnering with a technology support provider who focuses on the healthcare industry and has a deep level of understanding and commitment to help the healthcare provider reduce costs and improve their quality of care.

Perhaps the biggest concern is in the area of security. For healthcare organizations in particular, there are certain legal obligations such as those found in the HIPAA guidelines that must be fulfilled, otherwise the organization could face very heavy fines. In fact, these fines range anywhere from $100 to $50,000 per violation and up to $1.5 million dollars annually. These fines are becoming increasingly prevalent as the government steps up their auditing practices and are a real danger to the reputation and sustainability of most small businesses. As such, partnering with a consulting company who is not familiar with the healthcare organization's security obligations or their own obligations when doing business together can put both organizations in serious financial and legal risk.

In May of 2014 the New York-Presbyterian Hospital along with the Columbia University Medical Center agreed to pay nearly $5 million in fines to settle alleged HIPAA violations (HIPAA fine., 2014). Following an investigation it was revealed that a CU physician who developed applications for NYP mistakenly caused this breach. Under current law, when entities participate in joint compliance arrangements, they each share the burden of addressing the risks to protected health information (HIPAA fine., 2014).

In another unfortunate story, a Dentist in the Indianapolis area permanently lost his license when he mishandled the destruction of patient reports. These stories and countless others like them demonstrate the importance of having a technology support partner who understands these risks well and underscores the potential financial implications that could occur if the organizations do not have a strong understanding of the risks and obligations when entering into an outsourcing arrangement.

7.2: Benefits of Outsourcing Technology Support

Benjamin Franklin once said that "an ounce of prevention is worth an ounce of cure." The traditional approach to technology support is to just wait for problems to occur and simply contact a technology engineer to solve said problem. Typically, this work would be charged at some agreed upon hourly rate and would focus specifically on fixing only that particular problem. This is known in the technology support industry as the "break-fix" model. While this seems very cost-effective for some business leaders, this philosophy is wrought with potential issues.

The first problem is that this model does not provide any incentive for the IT support provider to do anything proactively to prevent these problems from occurring in the first place and more importantly, it leaves systems neglected for long periods of time, making the organization exponentially more vulnerable to security threats and attacks. In one study, it was found that on average, hackers were present on a company network for over 200 days before they were discovered. For healthcare providers in particular, this is disturbing. The safest and most effective way to mitigate the risk of a breach is through regular monitoring and updating with a proactive approach to support. A predictable, cyclical financial arrangement with an outsourcing provider allows the organization to budget their IT expenses reliably and take care of issues before they occur. While the alternative may be several months of no IT expense, you are bound to hit another month where thousands of dollars are needed to address an issue that could have been prevented. In other words, you will ultimately end up paying for a pound of "cure" for something that could have very easily been avoided with an "ounce" of prevention.

Although there are certainly major costs to consider when deciding to outsource technology support there are many benefits and a return on investment to consider as well. Perhaps the biggest reason for any organization to outsource IT is the potential for significant cost reduction. In fact, research has shown that more than 70% of respondents in one survey cited reduction of operating expenses as a key motivator behind outsourcing (Han, & Mithas, 2013). While the obvious cost savings when outsourcing IT may seem limited to just this area of the business, there are indications that outsourcing has downstream effects on other parts of the business as well. Financial models have suggested that IT outsourcing is negatively associated with non-IT operating costs. In other words, the indication is that for every one-unit increase in IT outsourcing as a percentage of revenue, a "1.26-unit decrease is found in non-IT operating costs" (Han, & Mithas, 2013, p. 7).

As noted earlier, some larger organizations may choose to outsource only a portion of their total internal IT support team. There are many cases that point to cost savings when outsourcing only the help desk, for instance. One study related to help desk outsourcing found that these outsourcing arrangements are having success in reducing expenses and noted "about 41% of organizations say their cost is less" under this arrangement (Help Desk., 2014, p. 6).

While cost benefits are often cited as the primary reason to outsource technology support, there are other significant benefits to consider as well. MALOVEC, S. N., BORYCKI, E. M., &

KUSHNIRUK, A. W. (2015) conducted a survey of organizations which had outsourced their information technology support and found that the benefits centered around qualitative as opposed to quantitative or financial benefits. Participants cited benefits around improved outcomes and service delivery which allowed healthcare providers to deliver services faster and more efficiently. This is consistent with previously stated findings that indicated downstream benefits in other key areas of the business, outside of just technology.

Adventist HealthCare in Gaithersburg, Md., outsources nearly half of its IT functions and depends primarily on outsourcing and consulting partners to provide services such as desktop support, telecommunications support, asset management, engineering and consulting, and equipment purchasing for thousands of workstations and multiple facilities (Health systems., 2015). Adventist indicated that these outsourced functions provide more security, greater flexibility and more resources to ensure continuous quality of care while at the same time driving strategic improvements and efficiencies.

7.3: A Cost-Benefit Case Study

For an accurate cost-benefit analysis, I have expressed costs and benefit numbers based on the operations of a local Indianapolis healthcare organization. Table 1 reflects costs for housing a full internal IT support staff based on a local Indianapolis-based healthcare organization. If the healthcare organization were to decide to outsource internal technology support for the infrastructure, Table 2 and Table 3 would reflect the net benefit in dollars as well as the benefit-cost ratio. Under this scenario, a technical liaison (Chief Information Officer) would be retained to represent the best interests of the organization, along with 3 application support specialists to continue managing more specialized applications that are unique to the organization. The organization would reduce staff from 10 to 4, removing the entire helpdesk staff, system administrator, network administrator, and IT Director. This service would also remove the cost of at least two monitoring systems that IT outsourcing companies typically provide as part of their service.

Table 1: Outsource Infrastructure

	Practice Cost and Revenue			*Outsourcing Cost Estimate*		
Cost Category	**Number of FTEs**	**Cost Per FTE**	**Total Cost**	**Monthly Support**	**Count**	**Annual Cost**
Labor				Computers	300	$162,000.00
Helpdesk	3	$ 50,000.00	$150,000.00	Servers	100	$180,000.00
Application Support Specialist	3	$ 80,000.00	$240,000.00	Networking Equipment	20	$ 7,200.00
System Administrator	1	$ 80,000.00	$ 80,000.00			
Network Administrator	1	$105,000.00	$105,000.00			
IT Director	1	$125,000.00	$125,000.00			
CIO	1	$200,000.00	$200,000.00			
Technology						
Network Monitoring Software			$ 5,000.00			
Desktop Antivirus			$ 5,000.00			
Total			**$ 1,015,000.00**	**Total**		**$ 349,200.00**

Table 1 represents staff salaries within a local Indianapolis-based healthcare organization. These salaries are derived from research of the organization and alignment with average salaries based on job titles and job responsibilities. Outsourcing costs for technology support were based on several quotes and estimates obtained from IT consulting companies. Total staff and associated costs for internal IT support, along with costs for obtaining specific technology outsourcing services are provided.

Table 2: Infrastructure Support Net Benefit

All Infrastructure Support (Net Benefit)			
Outsourcing IT Support	Benefit	$	470,000.00
	Cost	$	(349,200.00)
	Net	$	120,800.00

Table 2 outlines the net benefit for the outsourcing of all infrastructure support to an external outsourcing provider. The benefit amount of $470,000.00 reflects the savings in staff salaries, while the cost reflects the actual cost of outsourcing to an external third party.

Table 3: Infrastructure Support Benefit-Cost Ratio

Table 3

	All Infrastructure Support (Net Benefit)		
Outsourcing IT Support	Benefit	$	470,000.00
	Cost	$	(349,200.00)
	Ratio	$	1.35

The benefit-cost ratio is the represented in Table 3 and outlines the value of benefits over the value of costs associated with outsourcing for the first year. As the table shows, the first-year benefit cost ratio is 1.35 and indicates that for every dollar invested in outsourcing technology support, $1.35 will be earned.

7.4: Other Considerations

Apart from just the numbers alone, there are other considerations to take into account when deciding to outsource technology support services to an external third party. Access to additional personnel becomes an advantage under this scenario. Instead of relying solely on the limited amount of staff within the technology department, outsourcing this service provides access to many more support staff, available around the clock. Increased flexibility and ability to adapt to changes in technology is a likely benefit when outsourcing technology support. Proactive monitoring of servers and security patching is another key advantage to outsourcing. This work can happen in the background, allowing the business to focus on other, more strategic technology projects.

Considerations against outsourcing are primarily related to cost, security, accountability, legal and liability issues. While there are many technology consulting organizations willing to offer their services to the healthcare community, care must be taken to do the proper due diligence and ensure the consultant is familiar with the particulars of the industry from a patient safety, security, and legal point of view. Otherwise, there is an increased risk of significant legal and financial penalties for both the healthcare organization and the technology consulting firm. Additional costs to the organization are related to in-house expertise. By outsourcing support to an external party, there is the risk of partnering with a company or with technology engineers who are not as familiar with the particular inner workings of the healthcare company and the unique workflows, policies, and procedures the company relies on. When possible, healthcare organizations may consider retaining a technology liaison to work directly with the outsourcing partner to help maintain the best interests of the organization or by partnering with technology support providers who focus more specifically on the healthcare industry.

Section 8:

So What's Best for Healthcare Companies?

Healthcare organizations are challenged with new laws and regulations that put heavy demands on them to become more technology capable and financially responsible when it comes to promoting and sustaining patient outcomes and quality of care. In order to keep up with changing technologies and regulations, healthcare organizations increasingly look toward outsourcing as a potential strategy.

As we learned, there are a great number of healthcare organizations in the Indianapolis and surrounding areas. A significant percentage of those are either considering outsourcing some portion of their business or are currently doing so. Likewise, there are a great number of technology consulting companies in the area but a limited number that specifically focus on the healthcare community. Those that do promote services to the healthcare community often do not demonstrate an understanding of their responsibility and legal liabilities when servicing this industry.

Unlike larger healthcare organizations with big budgets and existing technology staff, smaller, independent providers have struggled in particular to keep up with changes in legislation and in technology. These private practitioners have been forced, in many cases, to sell their business or affiliate with a larger healthcare organization in order to survive. The purpose of this book and associated research was to enhance the healthcare industry's understanding of the various costs and benefits associated with outsourcing technology support and the need for more healthcare-specific IT consulting companies that are equipped to adequately service these organizations.

A review of the literature uncovered the many challenges facing the healthcare industry in relation to changes in technology and the increasing demands placed on these organizations to improve the quality of care through the adoption and integration of complex technology solutions. The number of healthcare organizations in Indianapolis alone was determined to be quite large, while the number of healthcare-specific technology consulting companies was determined to be quite small.

Different types of outsourcing strategies were identified to include the outsourcing of specific functions within IT, cloud-based services, and outsourcing of other "non-core" functions or business units. Likewise, the option to not outsource any of the technology support within the organization was considered.

This book is the culmination and analysis of data from several different sources in order to develop the costs and benefits associated with outsourcing technology support within the healthcare industry. Demographic data for the Indianapolis area was collected to determine an estimated number of healthcare organizations along with an estimated number of healthcare-specific technology consulting companies in typical metropolitan areas. A anonymous, Indiana-based healthcare company, was used to calculate average costs for internal IT support. Support costs for IT consulting providers were generated from cost averages based on first-hand experience with fees and quotes from various technology consulting companies. Costs considered included annual fees imposed by these technology consulting firms to manage the infrastructure of typical organizations. This would include managing desktop computers, servers, and networking equipment to maintain the basic technology infrastructure needs of the organization. The benefits for outsourcing technology support include the cost savings on the part of the healthcare organization through reduction of internal technology support staff. The net benefits were outlined along with the cost-benefit ratio.

8.1: What I Recommend

Based on the literature and the analysis conducted, the following are a set of recommendation for healthcare professionals considering outsourcing some or all of their technology needs for their practice:

1. Prior to making a decision to outsource, the healthcare organization should conduct a thorough cost-benefit analysis for their particular organization before determining whether this strategy is best for the organization.

2. Development of a communication strategy must be implemented in order to ensure any staff impacted by such a decision are treated in an ethical and fair manner.

3. Proper research and due-diligence by the healthcare organization into the credentials of the technology support provider must be completed to ensure the consultant is knowledgeable of the industry, experienced in supporting the industry, and understanding of their legal liability and accountability for keeping patient data protected.

4. Ensure that when entering into an agreement with a business partner, such as a technology support provider, that a Business Associate Agreement is completed and that the partner is compliant with HIPAA security mandates.

5. So much of the HIPAA security mandate can be met with a proactive approach to technology support. Healthcare leaders should put an emphasis on proactive monitoring and support to ensure systems are patched regularly, backups are monitored and tested, anti-virus definitions are

regularly updated, and security risks are assessed at least annually. These are all HIPAA requirements and if outsourcing IT is done by "your cousin Eddy", on an as needed basis, you risk serious financial and legal consequences. In other words, the days of the break-fix model, provided only when things break and by an individual or individuals with no industry experience, no HIPAA policies and procedures, and no Business Associate Agreement in place, are long over.

6. Partner with technology support providers who emphasize security. We have all heard the stories of Target, Anthem, and Sony but more and more, hackers are realizing that smaller organizations are softer targets and healthcare companies in particular, have exactly the type of information they are looking for.

7. Look for technology support providers who have a broad portfolio of services. While specialization is a good thing, you can save time and money by reducing the number of vendors that you are working with, which also reduces your risk. The fewer the number of people that have access to your sensitive data, the better.

8. Insist that your technology support provider offer monthly, quarterly, and/or annual business reviews to identify critical issues and remain in alignment

with your business. After all, if your plan is to have a partner that can support your systems in an instant, they will be much more effective if they remain intimately familiar with the continuous evolution of your business.

9. Take care to choose a partner that is responsive. Ask for service level agreements (SLA) where possible to help guarantee quality of service and availability. Partner with organizations of have a local presence whenever possible, as you are likely to receive more personalized and timely support.

10. Partner with technology support providers that have significant experience and a focus on your industry. Many technology support providers will have healthcare clients in their portfolio but often they are a smattering among a multitude of other clients from different industries. It is nearly impossible for any single organization to keep up with all of the regulatory, technological, and operational trends of multiple different industries. Partner with a company who has focus.

8.2: Conclusions

The cost-benefit analysis provided in this research has demonstrated that outsourcing the technology infrastructure support in a healthcare organization with existing technology support staff can be a sound financial decision. Through outsourcing the infrastructure support, the organization outlined in this research would save $120,800 per year through reduction in salary and savings on some internal technologies that would no longer be needed. The savings provided here will allow the organization to put those dollars toward solutions to increase efficiencies that will contribute to improved outcomes and quality of care.

With the changing legislative landscape and increasing demands on the average healthcare provider, it is important to have the flexibility to adapt to changes in technology and in the law in order to ensure there is continued progress toward reducing healthcare costs and improving the quality of care. Patients are increasingly demanding technology solutions that will allow them to communicate with their doctors remotely, access their medical information on demand, and ensure their private healthcare information is adequately protected.

Many healthcare organizations throughout the country have experienced success when outsourcing some portion of their technology support in either a financial perspective or quality of care perspective. "Outsourced IT functions such as those used at Adventist, provide health organizations with the security, flexibility and resources to ensure continuous, quality care while driving strategic improvements throughout their health care system" (Health systems., 2015, p. 1).

The healthcare industry is no stranger to change, however recent changes in the law combined with unprecedented growth and evolution in the technology industry has forced the healthcare industry to re-think how they conduct business. For decades, healthcare organizations were forced to focus on getting patients through the system as quickly and efficiently as possible, with limited technology tools to help them do so. Now that the model has changed to focus on cost reduction, efficiencies, quality of care, and improved outcomes, these organizations have turned toward outsourcing as a strategy. While outsourcing technology services in particular can be a sound strategy, healthcare leaders must be cautious of who they partner with and do the homework necessary to ensure all stakeholder needs are met or risk damaging their reputation or the safety and privacy of their patients.

References

Bateman, T.S., & Snell, S.A. (2013). *Management: Leading and collaborating in a competitive world (10th ed.). New York, NY:* McGraw Hill Irwin.

Cheney C. Developing value-based models. *Healthcare Leadership Review* [serial online]. December 2015;34(12):1-10 10p. Retrieved from: CINAHL Complete, Ipswich, MA. Accessed March 13, 2016.

Collins, D. (2009). Essentials of business ethics. [CourseSmart version]. Retrieved from http://www.coursesmart.com

Eddy, N. (2014). IT Outsourcing Slowdown Suggests Internal IT Investment. *Eweek*, 1. Retrieved from: Corporate ResourceNet, Ipswich, MA. Accessed March 25, 2016.

Everest Group Forecasts 12 Percent Growth in Healthcare IT Outsourcing as Healthcare Providers Step Up Investments. (2016, January 28). *Financial Services Monitor Worldwide*. Retrieved from http://0-bi.galegroup.com.oak.indwes.edu/essentials/article/GALE|A441 611539/5fe6a1da3a3c759ece2488f618ba8dd1?u=indwesun

Evolution of Healthcare Informatics Standards. (n.d.). Retrieved March 18, 2016, from http://www.himss.org/library/interoperability-standards/Evolution-of-Healthcare-Informatics-Standards

Fontenot, S. F. (2014). The Affordable Care Act and electronic health care records: can technology help reduce the cost of health care?. *Physician Executive, 40*(1), 68-72. Retrieved from: MEDLINE Complete, Ipswich, MA. Accessed March 19, 2016.

Groups hit with record $4.8M HIPAA fine. (2014). Retrieved March 25, 2016, from http://www.healthcareitnews.com/news/group-slapped-record-hipaa-fine

Han, K., & Mithas, S. (2013). INFORMATION TECHNOLOGY
OUTSOURCING AND NON-IT OPERATING COSTS: AN
EMPIRICAL INVESTIGATION. *MIS Quarterly*, *37*(1), 315-331.
Retrieved from: Corporate ResourceNet, Ipswich, MA. Accessed
March 25, 2016.

Health systems find that outsourcing IT saves money, boosts productivity,
improves care. (2015). *H&HN: Hospitals & Health Networks*,
89(10), 21-21 1p. Retrieved from: CINAHL Complete, Ipswich,
MA. Accessed March 25, 2016.

Help Desk Outsourcing Not Widely Embraced, But Rising. (2014).
Computer Economics Report, *36*(1), 6-14.

HIPAA Omnibus Rule creates obligations that BAs must not ignore.
(2014). *Briefings on HIPAA*, *14*(2), 1-4 4p. Retrieved from:
CINAHL Complete, Ipswich, MA. Accessed March 14, 2016.

Horalek, P. (2014). Smart Technology Lessens Burdens of ACA
Compliance. *Benefits Magazine*, *51*(5), 32.

Hughes, R. L., Ginnett, R. C., & Curphy, G. J. (2012). *Leadership Enhancing
the lessons of experience*. (7th ed.) New York, NY: McGraw-
Hill/Irwin.

Jillapalli, R. K., & Jillapalli, R. (2014). A Prescription for Medical
Outsourcing Success in the Affordable Care Act Milieu. *Journal Of
Global Marketing*, *27*(5), 285-297.
doi:10.1080/08911762.2014.909552

Kutscher, B. (2012, September 1). Outsourcing continues to grow.
Retrieved March 24, 2016, from
http://www.modernhealthcare.com/article/20120901/MAGAZI
NE/309019954

MALOVEC, S. N., BORYCKI, E. M., & KUSHNIRUK, A. W. (2015).
An Evaluation of Health Information Technology Outsourcing
Success. *Studies In Health Technology & Informatics, 208*253.
doi:10.3233/978-1-61499-488-6-253. Retrieved from: Publisher
Provided Full Text Searching File, Ipswich, MA. Accessed March
25, 2016.

Manta.com. (n.d.). Retrieved March 21, 2016, from
http://www.manta.com

O'Rourke, J., IV. (2013). *Management Communication: A Case Analysis
Approach (3rd ed.).* Manufactured in the United States. Pearson
Education.

Parmar, P. (2015). Outsourcing non-clinical processes in the healthcare
industry: contributions to long term sustainability. *International
Journal Of Healthcare Management, 8*(2), 65-67.
doi:10.1179/2047970015Z.000000000123

Paul, R., & Elder, L., (2014). *Critical Thinking Concepts and Tools (7th ed.).
Tomales, CA:* The Foundation for Critical Thinking.

Perna, G. (2013). Does Health IT Have a Staffing Crisis?. *Healthcare
Informatics, 30*(7), 44-46 3p. Retrieved from: CINAHL Complete,
Ipswich, MA. Accessed March 14, 2016.

Pratt, M. K. (2008). Ethical Outsourcing. *Computerworld, 42*(17), 32-33.
Retrieved from: Corporate ResourceNet, Ipswich, MA. Accessed
March 20, 2016.

Pyrillis, R. (2014). Affordable Care Act Brings Differing Prognoses on
What It Means for Jobs. *Workforce, 93*(3), 16. Retrieved from:
Corporate ResourceNet.

Robeznieks A. Working to keep reform on track. A changing industry poses challenges for healthcare leaders across all sectors. *Modern Healthcare* [serial online]. August 26, 2013;43(34):6. Retrieved from: MEDLINE Complete, Ipswich, MA. Accessed March 13, 2016.

Rothaermel. (2015). *Strategic Management Concepts, 2nd Edition.* [VitalSource Bookshelf Online]. Retrieved from https://bookshelf.vitalsource.com/#/books/1259296172/

Serviere-Munoz, L., & Mallin, M. L. (2013). How Do Unethical Salespeople Sleep at Night? The Role of Neutralizations in the Justification of Unethical Sales Intentions. *Journal Of Personal Selling & Sales Management, 33*(3), 289-306. doi:10.2753/PSS0885-3134330304

Sheingold, B. H., & Hahn, J. A. (2014). The history of healthcare quality: The first 100 years 1860–1960. *International Journal of Africa Nursing Sciences, 1*, 18-22.

Silicon Valley's vision for healthcare: Better care, outcomes; lower costs. (2016). *Ophthalmology Times, 41*(2), 38-40 2p. Retrieved from: CINAHL Complete, Ipswich, MA. Accessed March 14, 2016.

Temkar, P. (2015). Clinical operations generation next... The age of technology and outsourcing. *Perspectives In Clinical Research, 6*(4), 175-178. doi:10.4103/2229-3485.167098. Retrieved from: Academic Search Complete, Ipswich, MA. Accessed March 13, 2016.

Worldwide. (2016). Worldwide IT Spending Will Reach $2.8 Trillion in 2019 with the Strongest Growth Coming from the Healthcare Industry, According to IDC. *Business Wire.* Retrieved from:

Business Insights: Essentials, Ipswich, MA. Accessed March 24, 2016.

ZIMLICH, R. (2015). Outsourcing surges in popularity. *Managed Healthcare Executive*, 11-22. Retrieved from: Business Source Complete, Ipswich, MA. Accessed March 21, 2016.